This book belongs to:

_____

_____

A catalogue record for this book is available
from the British Library

Published by Ladybird Books Ltd
27 Wrights Lane London W8 5TZ

A Penguin company

© Disney MMI

Based on the Pooh stories by

A.A Milne (copyright The Pooh Properties Trust)

LADYBIRD and the device of a Ladybird are trademarks
of Ladybird Books Ltd

"Can Tiggers climb trees?"
said Roo.
"Tiggers don't climb trees,"
said Tigger. "They bounce
them!"

So Tigger and Roo
bounced. They bounced
up, up, up to the top
of the tree.

Tigger looked down.
"Tiggers don't like trees,"
he said.

Along came Tigger's
friends.

"Tigger is stuck," said Ro

"Can you get him down?

Christopher Robin took
off his coat.
Roo jumped down.

"Come on, Tigger," said Christopher Robin. "Jump down."

"Tiggers don't jump,"
said Tigger.
"They bounce."

18

And that's just what
they did!

OWL's